The Beasts of Blackwater

J. A. Henderson ■ Dynamo

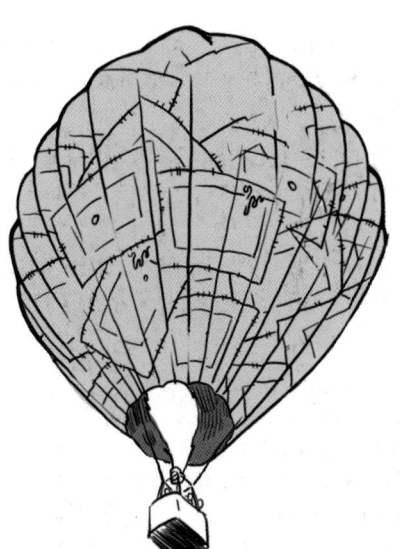

OXFORD
UNIVERSITY PRESS

TEAM X

Max, Cat, Ant and Tiger are four ordinary children with four extraordinary watches. When activated, their watches allow them to shrink to micro-size.

MAX
- hologram communicator

CAT
- magni-scope
- tracking device

ANT
- flip-up camera
- video recorder

TIGER
- warning light
- torch

Previously ...

The watches were running low on power. Ant tried to recharge them using a machine that he had invented. However, during this process, something in the watches changed irrevocably.

When all the watches are synchronized, the micro-friends can travel through a rip in the fabric of space and time to other dimensions. Max, Cat, Ant and Tiger have become *rip-jumpers*.

Unfortunately, there is a problem. The rip has become permanently stuck open ... in Tiger's wardrobe! This leaves Earth – our Earth – open to attack.

A woman called **Perlest** came through the rip saying she wanted to help. She told the children that they needed to find the **Weaver**. Only he could seal the rip shut forever.

After many rip-jumps, the micro-friends found the Weaver, otherwise known as **Aracnan**. They took him back to their dimension. But it had all been a trick! The woman they knew as Perlest turned out to be her evil twin sister **Vilana**. She stole the Weaver's **Staff of Worlds**.

Now the children are trying to hunt down Vilana before she can use the Staff of Worlds to free her master, **Mordriss**, *The Dimension Reaper*.

Chapter 1 – A growl in the dark

Max, Cat, Ant and Tiger stepped cautiously through the rip and found themselves in the shadow of a large granite overhang, slick with water and covered in damp moss. The last rays of the setting sun were dwindling over the horizon.

'This appears to be the exact rip Vilana came through,' Cat informed her friends, looking at the tracker on her watch. 'It looks like I've finally managed to synchronize the rips – we must be getting close. Although her signal's disappeared now.'

They looked around. There was no visible sign of Vilana. Moorland stretched away on all sides, dull and flat and nondescript. The silhouettes of similar outcrops dotted the landscape like jagged teeth jutting out of the gloom. A thick mist was rolling in.

'Great.' Tiger sighed, looking down at his feet. 'I'm standing in a puddle. Just once, I'd like us to appear on a sunny beach, with hammocks slung between palm trees. Is that too much to ask?'

'I don't like this at all.' Ant glanced behind him.

'It looks as if a good sneeze could bring that outcrop down on top of the rip. Hang on – the rip … it's … it's still open.'

'Ant, what's going on? Why hasn't the rip closed behind us?' Max asked, the concern written across his face.

Ant looked perplexed. 'I don't understand. It's not done that before. I can only think it's becoming more unstable the further we chase Vilana through the multiverse. She's created so many new rips with the Staff of Worlds, I guess it was just a matter of time before it started to have an effect on our rip-jumping.'

'Then we need to find Vilana and soon,' Tiger said. 'But where do we start? All the scenery looks the same, and it would be easy to get lost in this fog.'

'We'll just have to be careful.' Max took a couple of decisive steps and promptly disappeared headlong into a ditch. Seconds later, he re-emerged, dirty, drenched and rubbing his leg.

'What was that about being careful?' asked Cat.

'Must've tripped in a rabbit hole,' Max said, sheepishly. He picked some moss off his sleeve.

Tiger sniggered. 'Yeah, thanks for showing us what *not* to do.'

Max turned to Cat, red-faced. 'Any sign of Vilana?'

'I'm still not getting anything,' Cat said, checking the tracker on her watch. 'It's possible that all this mist might be interfering with my signal.'

'Well we can't hang about hoping the mist will clear. We'll scout around the immediate vicinity.' Max set off at a brisk jog with the others in pursuit.

After a few hundred metres, they came to a dirt track.

'At least there's some trace of civilization,' Max said. 'Let's follow it.'

'The mist is getting thicker,' Tiger cautioned, as the path wound between two low hills. 'Anyone else thinking this is a great place for an ambush?'

'Aw, don't be so paranoid,' Cat said with a grin. 'We only just got here.'

'For once, I agree with Tiger.' Ant's head swivelled from left to right as he tried to look in all directions at once. 'I really think we should go back.'

'Just a little further,' Max said, with a confidence he didn't feel. 'Don't worry, Tiger's watch will warn us if there's danger around.'

'Ehhhmmmm … there's danger around.' Tiger held up his wrist, showing his friends the red light flashing on his watch.

From somewhere to their left there was a low growl.

'Freeze, everyone!' Max hissed.

They stood stock still. In the echoing silence, they caught the faint scrabble of claws on rock and a soft, almost inaudible, panting. Whatever it was seemed to be trying to circle behind them.

'I think we're being hunted,' Ant whispered, sweat trickling down his neck. 'What shall we do?'

'Just stay still,' Cat warned. 'We don't know what we're up against.'

'We can't just stand here all night.' Tiger slowly pointed his watch in the direction of the sound. 'Maybe it's just a stray dog and it's too wary to come any closer. One way or another, we have to see what's out there.'

He activated the torch on his watch and a shaft of light sliced through the mist. The friends gasped in horror.

A hideous creature was revealed, squinting in the torch beam. It stood on two legs and was clothed in rags, but there all resemblance to a human ceased. Its skin was mottled with patches of coarse fur that sprouted from hunched, muscular shoulders. Long, powerful arms ended in hands that displayed sharp talons. And the face! A wolf-like muzzle, filled with vicious fangs, was topped by baleful yellow eyes.

With a cry of fear, Tiger concentrated the beam towards the creature's eyes, temporarily blinding it. The monster opened its salivating maw and roared in fury, before bounding away.

'Switch it off!' Cat screamed. 'There might be more of them around and you can see that light for miles!'

The light was extinguished.

'Calm down,' Tiger muttered. 'I scared it away, didn't I?'

In the distance they heard another roar. Then another. And another. All converging on the children. 'On the other hand ...' He blanched. 'I may have been a little hasty.'

'Don't panic.' Max tried to sound reassuring. 'The simple solution is to shrink and hide inside a rabbit hole. The whole moor is pockmarked with them.'

Before Max could blink, the others activated their watches, shrank and darted into the nearest burrow. Max reached for his wrist to do the same and gave a cry.

His watch wasn't there.

He looked wildly around him but he'd already guessed what had happened. It must have come off when he fell into the ditch near the rip.

A chill wind billowed around him, clearing the mist for a second, and Max caught sight of a stunted tree on top of a rocky hillock. Holding his breath he began to inch towards it, hoping the creatures were still too wary to attack.

Inside the burrow, Tiger switched on his torch and crawled deeper into the tunnel, pushing away loose stones and protruding roots. Trickles of dirt dropped from the roof and splattered on his face. He wiped at his eyes, trying to remove the grit.

'It's getting pretty narrow ahead. But I think we're deep enough to be safe.'

He looked over his shoulder. Cat and Ant were bunched behind him, their faces a mask of grime.

'Eh … guys? Where's Max?'

'Isn't he behind us?' Cat span round. 'Max?'

Ant, at the rear, managed to turn first. He scurried back to the entrance, kicking up clouds of dust, and pulled himself out of the hole.

Through the gap in the mist he could see Max backing uphill towards the tree, surrounded by shadowy shapes. Cat and Tiger appeared at Ant's shoulder.

'What is he *playing* at?'

'There must be something wrong with his watch.' Cat chewed her knuckle. 'We have to help him.'

'OK.' Tiger reacted first. 'Back to normal size and make as much noise as you possibly can.'

The children quickly grew to normal size and charged towards the hillock, screaming and waving their arms, stumbling over uneven ground and sending up splashes of muddy water. Out of the corner of their eyes, they could see the misshapen shadows melting away, accompanied by a cacophony of guttural grunts. They knew it was a temporary reprieve – the beasts would certainly be back.

Ant felt solid stone under his feet and groaned inwardly. The hillock was actually a granite slab, with the withered tree poking through a small crack. No rabbit holes to hide in here. They were completely exposed.

'What are you doing?' Spotting the others, Max tried to wave them away. 'I've lost my watch! You've got to get back to safety.'

'Yeah, right. As if!' Tiger reached him first. 'I'm still not abandoning you.'

'I don't leave a friend behind,' Ant added.

'Me neither,' Cat insisted.

Max clenched his fists. 'This is all my fault. How could I have lost my watch? We'll never be able to rip-jump again. That means we'll never find Vilana or get the Staff of Worlds back. I have to find my watch.'

'Stop beating yourself up.' Cat looked around her. 'I think we have more urgent things to worry about ... namely things with big, pointy teeth!'

Max snapped off a branch from the tree and stepped back against a large boulder to avoid being attacked from behind. 'Arm yourselves as best you can.'

The others followed suit. Then they waited, makeshift cudgels clutched in their hands.

'Come here, hoomansssss,' a sinister voice drifted out of the gloom. 'Lay down your weaponsssss.'

'They can speak!' Cat gave a shudder. 'But I don't think I want to listen.'

'We'd ask you to do the same,' Tiger shouted back. 'Only you seem to be quite attached to those talons of yours.' He smiled at the others. 'Attached. You get it? That was pretty funny, I thought.'

'Do not mock usssss,' the voice roared.

'Or we will slice you to bitsssss,' another creature said.

'I guess that's the peace talk over,' Ant grunted. 'Thanks for the input, Tiger.'

'Like they were going to offer us tea and scones,' Tiger retorted.

At that moment the clouds parted, revealing a bright moon. In the light, the friends saw a dozen glowing yellow eyes peering at them. The creatures had formed a circle round the children's dubious sanctuary.

Tiger's watch was flashing madly. 'Yeah, yeah,' he grunted, switching off the warning function. 'I think we're well aware of our situation.'

'Try your torch again,' Max said. 'Let's see exactly what we're up against.'

The dazzling white beam cut through the gloom, as Tiger swept his wrist in an arc.

The children were surrounded by a mass of snarling beasts, all slinking towards them. Each monster recoiled as the beam touched them, throwing hairy arms over their misshapen faces and howling in anger.

'I liked it better when we *couldn't* see what we were up against,' Ant wailed.

'They're blinded by the light,' Cat shouted. 'Keep waving it around, Tiger.'

The creatures retreated, momentarily dazzled. But, a few minutes later, they were creeping back, eyes cast down to avoid the glare of the torch.

'They're obviously intelligent,' Ant moaned. 'They know the light isn't an actual weapon.'

'Then we'll fight with what we have.' Max held up his arm. 'Pathetic sticks at the ready, everyone.'

The children bunched together, holding their sticks in front of them. Sensing victory, the beasts rose up and skulked towards the group, grinning wickedly and yelping animatedly to one another.

Chapter 2 – **Blackwater Hall**

'What's that noise?' Ant put a hand to his ear. 'It sounds like … hoof beats.'

The sound rose in volume and now the children could hear the jangle of harnesses and the creak of wooden wheels. The monsters whirled round as a carriage pulled by five grey horses crested the rise and thundered along the dirt track towards them. The driver was a thin man with a top hat and frock coat; he was holding a bull-whip above his head.

'I thought I saw illumination up here,' he announced to the friends, as the carriage slowed to a halt. 'Good show staying alive so far!'

He rose up from his seat and flipped a switch on a huge contraption next to him. 'As it happens, I have a light, too, though it's a bit larger.'

A piercing fluorescent beam lit the whole scene and the monsters backed away, hissing and spitting. One, larger than the rest, rushed blindly towards it and the man cracked his whip in an arc. The creature recoiled with a cry and fled back into the darkness.

'It seems to me you youngsters are sorely in need of assistance.' The stranger beckoned to the quaking group. 'Please avail yourselves of my transportation, *tout de suite.*'

'What did he just say?' Tiger frowned.

'He said *get in*,' Ant replied.

'And quickly, unless you want to end up as supper for the beasts,' the man urged.

Max, Cat, Ant and Tiger didn't need a second invitation. They bolted for the carriage, while the creatures were still disorientated by the light, and piled in. The stranger cracked his whip again and the horses took off, hooves churning up the dirt track.

The beasts screeched in anger and launched a new attack, bounding alongside the vehicle and clawing at

the doors in an attempt to get in. There was a rattle on the handle. Max leaned out of the window and swiped his stick down towards a snarling snout. Howling with pain, the creature dropped back.

The man driving the carriage shouted to the team of horses, 'Yaa!' The horses thundered forward faster than before and, one by one, their pursuers dropped away. They galloped along the path, which was now descending steeply into a valley. Ant looked out of the window and gulped as the edge of the precipitous path crumbled, sending a shower of dirt and stones down the side of the valley. He sat back in the carriage and closed the curtain, praying that the horses were sure-footed.

At the bottom of the valley, the rough path turned into a gravel drive that led up to a four-storey mansion of red brick with tall, latticed windows, surrounded by high, stone walls. The carriage stopped at a metal gate topped by barbed wire and the driver jumped down, unlocked it and pushed the barrier open. He led the horses inside and pulled the team to a stop, but they didn't settle, scraping the ground in agitation until their master had locked the gate once more.

The children clambered shakily out of the carriage. Max rubbed his wrist where his watch should have been. He wondered how he was going to find it now they were even further away.

'Welcome to my humble abode.' The stranger doffed his top hat again. 'May I be so bold as to ask your names?'

'I'm Max.' He shook the man's hand. 'My friends are Cat, Ant and Tiger.'

'Delighted to make your acquaintance.' The man gave a small bow. 'My name is Dr Amadeus Fishbalm.' He pointed to the mansion. 'And this is Blackwater Hall, where I currently reside. Would you care for some refreshments?'

The children sat round an oak table, in a plush study filled with bookcases and deep leather couches, while Dr Fishbalm fetched them something to eat. He returned carrying a tray of soggy asparagus and cabbage on a silver plate.

'Tuck in,' he said, setting the platter in front of them. 'Everything is harvested from my own garden. I'm a bit of an amateur horticulturist.'

'Eh … a packet of crisps would have done.' Tiger poked at the overcooked greens in disgust.

'Crisps? Never heard of them I'm afraid. I stick with the vegetables.' The doctor shrugged. 'I do have some ten-year-old cans of prunes though …'

'This will do fine.' Cat nudged Tiger in the ribs.

Tiger reluctantly scooped a forkful of emerald gloop into his mouth and tried not to look queasy. 'Thank you very mush … I mean much.'

While they ate, Dr Fishbalm regarded the children with open curiosity. He was quite a sight himself. Tall and gangly, with a thin pencil line moustache, he wore a frock coat and spotted bow tie.

'Excuse my impertinence', he said finally, 'but how on earth did you end up on this island?'

So they were on an island. Ant made a mental note of that useful fact. The more he could find out about this dimension the better.

'We got here using the r–' Tiger began. Max gave him a swift kick under the table to shut him up.

'Ow!' Tiger rubbed his shin.

'Raft,' Ant quickly corrected. 'We got here using a raft. The sail broke and we've been drifting for a long, long time. So we don't know exactly where we've ended up.'

The others were happy to let Ant do all the talking. They knew he was quick-witted and would glean information about this new world without giving away that they were from another dimension.

'A raft?' Dr Fishbalm cocked his head. 'How on earth did you land? The only jetty is behind the hall. The rest of the island is ringed by jagged rocks and sheer cliffs.' He studied his nails nonchalantly. 'Is the craft still … intact?'

'It … eh … broke up on the rocks,' Ant lied. 'Took us hours to climb the cliff. Then we got lost on that moor.'

'And I apologize for the reception you received,' the doctor said regretfully. 'But you are safe here. Well … fairly safe.' He glanced at the clock on the wall. 'It's rather late. Perhaps you would like to retire for the night and we can get to know each other better tomorrow?'

'That's a great idea.' Tiger gave a yawn. 'Running for my life has tired me out.'

Max scratched his lip thoughtfully. He was desperate to get on with the mission, and he couldn't see any evidence that Vilana was even still in this dimension. On the other hand, he and his friends were exhausted and he didn't much relish the idea of going back out in the dark with those creatures on the loose. Surely one night in a soft bed wouldn't do any harm?

'Thank you, Dr Fishbalm,' he said gratefully. 'We'd be delighted to accept your hospitality.'

'I have trouble sleeping.' Ant quickly scanned the bookshelves. 'Could I borrow something to read? That always helps.'

'By all means, take whatever strikes your fancy,' said Dr Fishbalm, nodding agreeably. 'There's a very interesting book on furniture polish that I often read before bed.'

'This will do.' Ant grabbed a slim volume from the shelf.

Dr Fishbalm lit a candle, escorted them up a flight of stairs, opened a heavy iron door and ushered them inside.

The children found themselves in a stone room with four iron bunks. In a small adjoining alcove was a porcelain sink and a toilet.

'I shall ring a bell at breakfast time. There are

towels and night things in the cupboard.' The doctor bowed and backed out into the hall. 'Until then, young travellers, nighty-night and don't let the beasts bite. Har har!'

The door creaked shut. Ant sat in a hard, wooden chair, lit a candle on the table beside him and began to read, while the others took in their surroundings.

'This place is weird,' Max commented. 'What kind of house has bedrooms with iron doors? And there are bars on the windows.'

'Probably to keep those monsters out,' Cat replied. 'This is a different dimension, remember? Things are bound to be a bit odd.'

'Dr Fishbalm certainly is.' Ant looked up. 'Those vegetables were seriously overcooked!'

'I'm so tired I'd sleep in the sink if I had to.' Tiger was already face down on the nearest bed. 'This is comfier though.' Within a few seconds he was snoring gently.

'You don't have trouble sleeping either, you big liar.' Cat leaned over Ant's shoulder. 'What are you up to?'

'I spotted this in Dr Fishbalm's library and wanted an excuse to look at it.' Ant held up the book's cover.

A Short History of the Continent was printed on the front in gold letters. 'We can't tell a complete stranger we're from another dimension, so we'd better find out about this place pronto before we give ourselves away. Luckily I'm a fast reader.'

And he was. By the time the others had got ready for bed, he had skimmed through most of the pages.

'Well?' asked Cat.

'Technology-wise,' Ant said, 'it's got steam trains, airships and boats, but nothing more modern than that.'

He turned to the last page and held up a map. 'The geography is different, too. See? There's a large central continent called Tolemeda, which contains hundreds of large cities and is quite advanced. But it's surrounded by thousands of small islands like this one … so many that a lot of them have never been properly explored.' He shut the book. 'If we pretend we're from one of those, we can plead ignorance about the whole area and won't have to mention the rip.'

'Anything in there about monsters like the ones we saw?' Cat shuddered.

'There are lots of legends about fantastical creatures,' Ant replied. 'Sea serpents. Faeries. Werewolves.' He bit his lip. 'Looks like, in this dimension, some of them are actually true.'

'That explains the fortifications.' Max looked out of the window at the huge wall surrounding them. The fog had finally lifted and, in the darkness beyond, he was sure he could see shadowy shapes moving round. 'It looks like it was built to keep out an army. But what is Dr Fishbalm doing here all on his own? I haven't seen any other humans around.' He shook his head. 'I don't like it. I don't like it at all.'

'In the morning we'll have breakfast with our host and find out if he's had any other visitors recently.' Ant got into one of the beds.

'You mean Vilana?' Cat said.

'Exactly. If there's no trace of her on this island, we'll just have to keep looking elsewhere.' He stretched. 'I must admit, it looks like a dead end to me.'

'How are we going to get back to the rip *and* find your watch, Max?' Cat asked. 'The island is crawling with creatures!'

'Good question.' Max frowned. 'I'm still working on that part.'

Chapter 3 – Stewed mutton

Breakfast consisted of greasy, sliced turnip and runner beans. Tiger gave a small groan. 'I'd rather face the monsters than eat another meal here,' he whispered to Cat. 'This guy may be an expert on horticulture but he's a rotten cook.'

'Plenty of seconds, if this doesn't fill you up.' Dr Fishbalm was tucking heartily into his plateful. 'It's so nice to have company for, as you may have guessed, I have the misfortune to be the only human left on Blackwater Island.'

'Yes, we were going to ask about that …' Max began.

'I have a few questions first.' The doctor pushed his plate away. 'Where exactly are you from?'

'We live on an island, too,' Ant said truthfully. 'It's very far away.'

'I'm a bit of an amateur geographer.' Dr Fishbalm daintily dabbed his lips with a napkin. 'What is the place you inhabit called?'

'Britain.'

'Never heard of it.'

'No. I doubt it's on any of your maps.'

'I do not wish to appear impertinent.' Dr Fishbalm fiddled with the tip of his moustache. 'But I suspect you are not telling me the whole story.'

'What makes you say that?' Ant asked nervously.

'Your outfits are made from a cloth I have never seen before.' The doctor pointed to their wrists. 'And I'm a bit of an amateur inventor. Enough to know those devices are far in advance of anything my world could produce.'

'I … eh …' Ant stammered. 'It's complicated.'

'But mainly, I know you are lying because the cliffs around Blackwater are completely unclimbable.' The doctor raised an eyebrow. 'If you have any strange means of transport on or off this island, then you must inform me. It's a matter of life or death.'

The children glanced guiltily at each other.

'Perhaps if I explained the situation here on Blackwater, you might trust me a little more. Although, I warn you, it is a terrible tale to tell.' Dr Fishbalm gave Cat an apologetic smile. 'I do not know if it is a story to recount when a lady is present, however, lest you have a swooning spell. I have no smelling salts to revive you.'

'I'm not the swooning type,' Cat said, through gritted teeth.

Dr Fishbalm shrugged. 'As you wish. Let me begin my story then. You see, Blackwater Hall is my home now.' Dr Fishbalm hunched forwards. 'But, at one time, it used to be a prison.'

That got the children's attention.

'Blackwater Jail was home to all manner of unsavoury and violent characters,' the doctor continued. 'I was the prison doctor, which I must admit, was an easy task. You see, the inmates became unspeakably healthy from the moment they were shipped here.' He lowered his voice conspiratorially. 'Too healthy in fact …'

'Must have been all those greens you serve up,' Tiger muttered.

Dr Fishbalm was impervious to his sarcasm. 'The garden was only large enough to feed myself and the wardens. The prisoners mainly ate mutton stew, for the island had a plentiful supply of sheep. But, while the prisoners seemed to flourish on their new diet, it eventually did something terrible to them.' He narrowed his eyes. 'They began to change.'

'Change?' asked Max, with a shudder. He had a feeling he knew what was coming next.

'They became more and more like beasts. They grew stronger and their senses got keener. Then, one night, the prison handyman went missing. All we found in his quarters the next morning was his cap and an empty bowl.' He sighed. 'Poor Mr Wattbottle. Such a nice man, but he was always partial to a bit of mutton. We could hear him howling outside the walls.'

'He changed, too?' Ant asked.

'Indeed. And he was the man who maintained the place and kept it running smoothly. With him gone, the wardens became most concerned, as you can imagine. The prison security systems began to fail – some of the automatic gates, the cameras, that kind of thing – and with the inmates becoming more violent, the wardens became fearful for their lives.'

'Then what happened?' Tiger leaned forwards in his chair.

'I sent the wardens away on the only boat we had with orders to alert the authorities to our appalling situation. They had instructions to quarantine the island until I gave the all clear.'

'Why did *you* stay?' Tiger asked.

'A doctor does not abandon his patients,' Dr Fishbalm bristled.

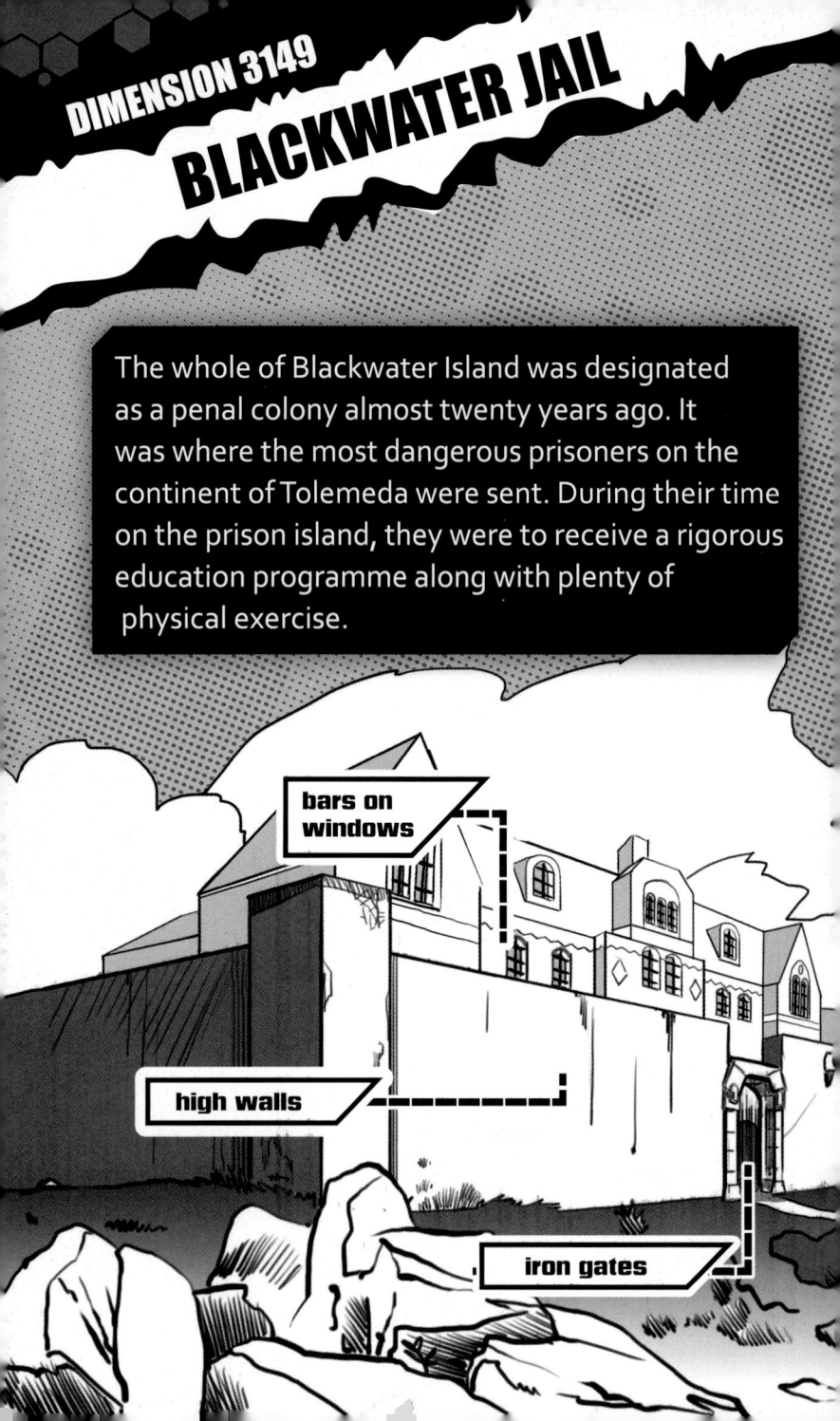

However, things didn't go quite as the authorities had planned. When the first wave of criminals was sent there – fifty of them in total – it wasn't long before the wardens reported changes in them. They became more aggressive and started to change in their appearance, displaying physical characteristics more akin to wolves. The twenty wardens on the island started to fear for their lives; they managed to escape and alert the authorities. The island was put into a state of indefinite quarantine.

No official has dared to set foot on the island since.

Dr Fishbalm ran his hands through his hair. 'I couldn't keep the prisoners in their cells for they were now completely wild. So I let them loose and hid in the infirmary until they were all gone.' The doctor leaned back in his chair and bridged his fingers. 'Then I barricaded myself in the prison to work on an antidote to their unfortunate condition.'

'Did you manage to develop one?'

'Of course. I already had the necessary skills.' Dr Fishbalm pointed proudly to a framed picture on the wall behind his chair. The photo was of a younger Dr Fishbalm. He looked like he was wearing a laboratory coat.

'I'm a bit of an amateur botanist, and I soon discovered there were tiny, yellow flowers on the island with quite astonishing transformational qualities. The sheep had been eating the flowers and, although they were immune to their effects, humans, obviously, were not. Once the prisoners began eating the meat from the sheep they started to change almost immediately. As soon as I worked that out, it was simple for a man of my skills to distil the flower pollen and devise a cure for their condition.'

'Modest, isn't he?' Tiger whispered to Cat.

'So why haven't you changed the prisoners back?' Max asked.

'How could I get them to drink it?' Dr Fishbalm looked crestfallen. 'Whenever I go outside these walls, the creatures try to tear me limb from limb. I can only make short trips in my carriage, and even those are fraught with danger, as you saw with your own eyes. The light I mounted on the carriage and my bull-whip can only keep them at bay for so long.'

'Can they get in here?' Tiger glanced around him.

'I dare say they could, if they really tried. But the walls here are high, I leave the beasts to their own devices and they have plenty of sheep to eat outside. So we have a stalemate, of sorts.'

He stood up from his chair. 'Or we did, until you arrived.'

'That sounds ominous.' Ant winced.

'Indeed.' The doctor tapped his emaciated fingers together. 'These abominations were once human, so do not underestimate their intelligence. They will be very curious about how you reached Blackwater. I have little doubt they are scouring the island as we speak, looking for whatever craft brought you here so that they can use it as a means of escape.'

'I told you, our raft broke up.' Ant was perspiring with the effort of his implausible lie.

'If that is true then they are thwarted.' Dr Fishbalm fondled his moustache. 'Unfortunately, they may decide it is now worth mounting an assault on the prison to interrogate you themselves.'

'I think we need to have a quick discussion.' Cat pulled Max to his feet. 'Would you please excuse us for a second, Dr Fishbalm?'

'Most certainly. I shall make us a nice spinach porridge while I wait.'

Chapter 4 – **Ambush**

The four children stepped out into the hallway.

'If those creatures find the rip and escape through it', said Cat anxiously, 'there's no telling where they'll end up, or the havoc they'll cause. I mean, what if they get through to our dimension?' She shuddered at the thought of the beasts getting anywhere near her home and family. 'We have to reach the rip first.'

'And then what?' Tiger asked. 'If we go through, there's a chance they could follow.'

'Perhaps the doctor could seal the rip behind us, if we told him about it that is.' Ant snapped his fingers. 'One stick of dynamite would bring down that rocky outcrop.'

'I don't know.' Max rubbed his temple. 'I've got an uneasy feeling about this Fishbalm guy. Something just doesn't smell right.'

'That's probably his overcooked cabbage,' Tiger guffawed.

'Are you kidding me?' Cat threw up her hands, exasperated.

'I'm just saying ...' Max began.

Cat didn't let him finish. 'He stayed behind to work on a cure for those prisoners, when everyone else abandoned them. He's a hero.'

'The wardens *didn't* abandon anyone. Fishbalm ordered them away,' Max said, not convinced. 'And he referred to the inmates as *abomination*s. That doesn't sound too caring.'

'I don't see that we have much choice but to tell him the truth,' Ant interrupted. 'With those monsters prowling out there, we'll never get back to the rip on our own. Like it or not, we need his help.'

'I suppose so.' Max was still uncertain.

'Then it's decided.' Cat opened the door and ushered her companions into the study where Dr Fishbalm was waiting for them.

'Dr Fishbalm. We have a story of our own to tell you ...'

Dr Fishbalm sat silently while the children recounted their tale, including how they had really reached Blackwater.

'Oh dear,' he said, when they had finished. 'Oh dear. Ohdearohdearohdear.' He stood up and paced the room. 'I have never encountered this Vilana woman you speak of. But we must get you back to that rip before the beasts find it. Fortunately, I'm a bit of an amateur chemist …'

'Told you,' Ant whispered, nudging Max.

'Is there anything you're not an amateur at?' Tiger said, smirking.

'Yes, I played professional hopscotch when I was a young man.' Dr Fishbalm scratched his head. 'Anyway, as I was saying, I've already whipped up a small batch of explosive liquid using baking soda and a few other ingredients I found lying around in the kitchen. I intended to use it as a defence against the creatures, but it will be equally efficient at bringing down any rocks above this rip of yours.'

'Have you got any ideas on how we can actually reach the rip, doctor?' asked Cat.

'Since time is of the essence, I propose we take the carriage. If we make a run for it soon, we can take our adversaries by surprise.' Dr Fishbalm clapped his hands. 'I see no need to delay. My steeds are well rested, and those fiendish creatures won't expect us to make another foray outside so soon. If we go now, we will surely catch them unawares.'

'Let's do it.' Tiger gave a grim smile. 'Do you have any other weapons … just in case?'

'I'm afraid we'll have to rely on speed alone. Let's not tarry, my youthful companions!' Dr Fishbalm strode off to the stables.

'So the wardens just left without him … on an island full of monsters, without any means to defend himself?' Max said to Cat.

'You said yourself,' Cat said defensively. 'Fishbalm ordered them to go.'

'I'm telling you, Cat. Something isn't right.'

The five grey horses pawed the ground impatiently as the children climbed into the carriage.

'Max? Kindly open the gate; then lock it behind you.' Dr Fishbalm, top hat set at a jaunty angle, patted the seat beside him. 'After that, you can ride up here with me. It's a lovely view, as long as you keep your eyes peeled for anything that might tear us apart.'

'Wow,' Max grunted. 'Don't give up your day job to become a tour guide.'

Once Max was safely aboard, Dr Fishbalm cracked his whip, and the horses trotted along the dirt path and up the hill towards the moor, feathered plumes bobbing on their heads. They crested the summit and broke into a canter.

'Cat?' Max thumped on the side of the vehicle. 'When we get close to the rip, can you use your tracker to guide us to the exact spot?'

'Will do,' Cat's voice drifted up.

'I was meaning to inquire about that.' Dr Fishbalm squinted at his passenger. 'What exactly are these watches capable of?'

Max didn't answer. He was staring ahead. 'Something's wrong with the horses,' he hissed.

The horses were tossing their heads from side to side, eyes rolling in panic.

'They've picked up the creatures' scent.' Dr Fishbalm's shoulders tensed.

'Wouldn't they have to be close by for that to happen?' Max gripped the side of the seat. 'I mean ... *really* close?'

'They're pretty smelly, even at a distance ... but, yes', the doctor's eyes darted from side to side, 'I do believe we have blundered into an ambush.'

He pulled on the reins and the horses skidded to a halt, sweat foaming on their muscular necks.

'Are we there yet?' Tiger shouted.

'We're going to have to turn back.' Dr Fishbalm tried to turn the carriage round, but the path was too narrow and the horses were snorting in alarm.

'Where are you, you horrible beasties?' The doctor stood up and shaded his eyes with one hand. Suddenly he paled. 'Oh dear. Oh dearohdearohdear.'

As if on cue, the creatures rose up all over the moor. They had been lying flat on their faces in the dirt, the brown bristles on their backs blending perfectly with the undergrowth. The lead horse reared up, whinnying in terror.

'No time to turn the carriage round now!' Dr Fishbalm leapt down and opened the carriage door. 'We'll be faster riding on the horses. Good job I invented a quick-release system on this harness. I'm a bit of an amateur saddler you know …'

He began unfastening the terrified animals from their rig as the monsters raced towards them.

'We have you now, hoomansssss,' one of them cried.

'I'm not much of a rider,' Tiger yowled, as Fishbalm gave him a leg-up.

'All you have to do is hold on!' The doctor quickly helped the others up on to their mounts.

Tiger clung to the horse's thick mane. 'But how do you steer?'

'Don't worry. The horses know the way back and, by the look of it, they're rather keen to get there!'

As the beasts bounded towards them, the horses wheeled round and raced back the way they had come, necks outstretched, breathing hard. Dr Fishbalm vaulted gracefully on to the back of the remaining steed and galloped after them. Within seconds, he was overtaking the children.

'Don't tell me ...' Max said with a groan. 'You're a bit of an ...'

'A bit of an amateur jockey, yes. How did you guess?' He waved to Max as his mount sped past.

Meanwhile, one beast, closer than the others, launched itself at Cat, claws outstretched. She folded forward, low over her horse's neck, and the creature soared over her head. It landed with a loud crunch and rolled into a spiky bush where it became entangled among the sharp thorns.

'Jolly good show!' Dr Fishbalm tipped his hat at her. 'You'd make a fine polo player, Cat.'

Another creature launched itself at the doctor. He stuck a booted foot into the snarling maw and the monster ploughed into the earth with a loud yelp.

Eventually they were leaving their pursuers behind. The creatures were fast but, once again, their speed was no match for the petrified horses. The party reached the gates of Blackwater Hall and thundered to a halt, well ahead of the baying pack. The children cantered inside and jumped down from their mounts, while Dr Fishbalm locked the gates behind them. As they looked around, Tiger was still clinging to the neck of his horse with his eyes closed.

'Er, Tiger,' said Ant.

'What?' he whimpered.

'You can let go now.'

Tiger opened one eye, then the other. He slid slowly off, knees buckling. 'That was … It was …'

'Fast?' said Cat.

'Exciting?' offered Ant.

'Absolutely terrifying,' corrected Tiger.

'Well, it was definitely quite an adventure.' Dr Fishbalm dusted off his hat, seemingly unconcerned by this brush with death. 'And it's almost lunchtime. Perhaps I can offer you some stewed broccoli while we come up with a new plan?' He patted his jittery horse affectionately. 'But first I must attend to my faithful steeds and see they are fed and watered.' He opened the stable doors and the horses trotted inside. 'The poor souls have had quite a scare.'

'*They've* had a scare!' Tiger looked at his trembling hands. 'I feel like I'm going to faint.'

'Then be careful not to land in the water trough!' the doctor said with a chuckle.

'He is altogether too cheerful about this,' Max wheezed. 'Something is *definitely* not right about him.'

Chapter 5 – **Plan B**

The children sat quietly, picking morosely at their overcooked vegetables. Only Dr Fishbalm ate heartily, humming softly to himself. Eventually, he sat back and pushed his plate away, staring at the other faces around the table.

'The creatures have changed their habits,' he said finally. 'They're normally nocturnal, but now they're obviously staying awake during the day as well. I think they've guessed that we're trying to find your means of transportation, and they're not going to rest until they find it, too.'

'And if they can't?' Max asked.

'As I said, I presume they'll mount an attack. It'll take them a while to work up to assault our fortifications. But, eventually, they'll come for us.'

'There must be another way to get to the rip,' Ant said to Cat. 'What if we attempted the journey at micro-size, using the heather for cover?'

Cat shook her head. 'It would be an awfully long walk if we were tiny. And Dr Fishbalm said the creatures' senses were heightened. They'd probably sniff us out. Besides, we're still a watch down remember.' She looked over at Max.

'Don't look so glum, my strangely-attired friends.' Dr Fishbalm raised his glass. 'It's true that we can't get past the beasts on land. So what does that leave?'

'We tunnel under them?' Tiger ventured. 'Should only take a few years.'

'Oh, I do like your sense of humour, young man.'

'I wasn't joking.'

'Why, it's simple,' Dr Fishbalm retorted with a hint of exasperation. 'We *fly* over them.'

'You have an aeroplane?' Ant gasped.

'What's an aeroplane?'

'Oh. I forgot they haven't been invented in this dimension.'

'But I *do* have a flying machine,' Dr Fishbalm countered. 'It's a hot-air balloon that I made by stitching the prison bed sheets together – no quick task, let me tell you. I also developed a concoction of ingredients to make the sheets somewhat less flammable. After that, it was just a matter of attaching the giant prison laundry basket underneath.'

'Don't tell me,' Tiger sighed. 'You're a bit of an amateur aviator?'

'Absolutely. Plus I have a lot of spare time on my hands.' Dr Fishbalm began to clear away the dishes. The children huddled together in the corner of the study.

'This guy is great,' Cat gushed. 'It's a pity we can't take him with us.'

'He built a hot-air balloon out of bed sheets,' Max said exasperated. 'I don't care how much spare time he has, doesn't anyone else think that's a bit weird?'

'You're just jealous.' Cat poked him. 'It seems there's nothing he can't do.'

'Exactly. So why was he working as a lowly prison doctor?'

'Because he cares, Max.' Cat insisted. 'He's one of life's truly good guys. Why can't you accept that?'

'Like I said before,' Ant stepped in hastily, 'we don't have much choice but to go along with his scheme.'

The children stood in the courtyard watching Dr Fishbalm prepare his hot-air balloon. He lit the burner that was fixed inside in the laundry basket. As the flames danced up, the friends helped him hold up the fabric until the whole thing began to inflate. Soon the giant balloon billowed high above them.

'Climb aboard, chaps.' Dr Fishbalm pulled himself into the basket. 'Then get ready to let go of the ballast.'

'You mean those socks filled with sand tied to the side?' Ant prodded one gingerly as he climbed in.

'Yes. And the sooner the better. They belonged to the prisoners, so they reek of unwashed feet.'

Soon all the children were inside, crammed shoulder to shoulder.

'It's rather a squeeze, I'm afraid,' Dr Fishbalm apologized. 'I wasn't expecting it to hold five.'

'That's obvious!' Max grunted. 'Tiger, get your elbow out of my ear.'

'How do you steer this thing?' Ant asked hesitantly.

'I built a little rudder.' Dr Fishbalm began untying the sand-filled socks and letting them fall. 'Hopefully it will work.'

'Wait. *What?*' Max grabbed his shoulder. 'Are you telling me you've never flown this before?'

'Not as such.' Dr Fishbalm let the last sock go.

'Oh, please.' Ant put his head in his hands. 'Just throw me out now.' He started to pale as the balloon jerked into the air.

'I'm getting out.' Tiger hooked one leg over the rim of the basket.

But it was too late. The huge balloon was already rising over the prison wall.

'Well, well.' Dr Fishbalm cried gleefully. 'It does work after all. Who knew?'

He twisted the rudder and the makeshift craft began to drift over the moor.

'There's a stiff breeze.' Dr Fishbalm licked a finger and held it up. 'We'll reach our destination long before our adversaries can get there. But where exactly are we going?'

'That way.' Cat studied the tracker on her watch and pointed. 'About five miles due south.'

'What a fascinating contraption.' The doctor's eyes lit up. 'May I examine it?'

'Just you keep steering,' Max commanded. 'Where are the explosives to bring down the outcrop?'

'Under my top hat, of course.'

'You are *kidding* me.' Ant groaned. 'Please don't sneeze.'

As they flew further out over the moorland, the basket began to wobble.

'The wind is changing direction,' Dr Fishbalm grimaced, struggling with the rudder. 'Are we still on the right course, young lady?'

Cat glanced again at her watch. 'Looks like it.'

'Then nothing can stop us!' The doctor glanced up. 'Eh … well, nothing but *that*.'

The others followed his gaze and gasped. Yellow flames were licking up one side of the sheets.

'The balloon is on fire!' Ant screeched.

'Ah, it seems my concoction to hinder the sheets catching fire needs some more work.'

'Really?' said Tiger sarcastically. 'I'd never have guessed.'

Dr Fishbalm pulled hard on the rudder. The balloon lurched round and began heading back towards Blackwater Hall. 'What an extremely trying day!'

By the time the prison appeared over the horizon, half the balloon was on fire; the basket was rapidly sinking and they were shrouded in acrid smoke.

'We're not going to make it over the wall!' Cat cried. 'And look what's under us.'

The others peered down. A dozen beasts were circling below them, licking their lips in anticipation.

'Then they're in for a surprise.' Dr Fishbalm calmly removed his hat, grabbed a bottle of clear liquid from inside it and dropped it over the side.

There was a huge explosion and the monsters scattered in fright.

As the burning balloon slowly draped itself over the prison wall, Dr Fishbalm called out, 'Brace yourselves!'

They all huddled together, muscles tense, as the basket swung against the outside of the prison wall. The occupants leapt from the basket; Dr Fishbalm opened the gate and they collapsed inside again.

'Well. We're back in prison,' Tiger groaned. 'Got any more great ideas, Dr Fishbalm?'

'Sorry about that.' The doctor propped himself up on one sooty elbow. 'I believe you mentioned digging a tunnel?' He coughed loudly. 'Only jesting. I'll think of something. Probably.'

Max glared at him. He was all too aware that Vilana was getting further away with every passing day, and they were no closer to finding her. And now Fishbalm was making jokes! He turned to Cat, who was choking and spluttering beside him. 'You may think he's a hero,' he said. 'But I'm *really* starting to dislike this guy.'

Chapter 6 – Rogues' gallery

Max, Cat, Ant and Tiger sat round the table fruitlessly trying to come up with another plan. Even Dr Fishbalm looked uncharacteristically solemn. Outside the sun was sinking over the horizon.

'I'm afraid I'm out of ideas to reach your rip,' the doctor said finally. 'So now we must plan our defence. I would advise you to retire early and get as much rest as possible, for I do not think the creatures will attack tonight.'

'Why not?' Tiger asked.

'I have set up large gas lights around the perimeter walls and, like all night hunters, they have very sensitive eyes. I imagine they will spend the hours of darkness looking for your transportation instead.'

Seeing their glum faces, Dr Fishbalm gave a reassuring smile. 'Never fear. The island is big and they are undoubtedly searching for a boat or an airship. It would never occur to them that you came through a portal from another dimension.' He scratched his temple. 'To be honest, I'm still getting *my* head round that one.' He drummed the table in thought. 'So … my guess is they'll attack in the morning.'

'And you have no weapons at all?' Max furrowed his brow.

'There's one vial of explosives left but we need that to bring down the overhanging rock over the rip,' the doctor apologized. 'I'll see what I can dig up. In the meantime, get yourselves to bed. You'll need all your strength for tomorrow.' He got up and stretched. 'I'll patrol the walls, just in case. Besides, the night air is bracing and will clear my head. I'm sure to think of something brilliant.'

'I have faith in you.' Cat began to clear away the dishes. 'Don't worry. We'll wash up.'

Back in their room, Max stared out of the window. He could see the lanky figure of the doctor pacing the ramparts, whistling to himself. Tiger was already snoring on his bunk.

'How can he sleep?' Ant grumbled. 'I can't … not knowing those things might be coming to get us at any moment.'

'Then come with me.' Max pulled open the door. 'Grab a couple of lanterns.'

'Dr Fishbalm said we should rest,' Cat said. 'Where are you going?'

'I want to look around, while your resident genius is out of the way. We've been here two days and he's never offered to show us the place.'

'Maybe he's been too busy risking his life trying to get us to the rip,' Cat snapped back.

'What can I say? I'm a bit of an amateur nosy-parker.' Max ignored Cat's dirty look. 'C'mon, Ant. You fancy a stroll?'

The two boys grabbed a lamp each and crept down endless, dim corridors, lined with cells.

'It's spooky as anything here.' Ant peered into one of the dingy cubicles. 'But Cat's right. It's just a prison. Fishbalm isn't hiding anything.'

'Wait. Here's the Head Warden's office.' Max pushed open a panelled door and entered the musty room. 'Let's see if there are any files on this place.' He tested a few of the dusty wooden cabinets. 'They're all locked.'

'You don't need files.' Ant lifted his lantern as high as he could. 'There's a rogues' gallery right here.'

Max looked up. Dozens of posters were tacked to the walls, an array of villains glaring down at them, each with a name and list of crimes.

INMATE 24

DIRK FILTHY.
CATTLE RUSTLING. LARCENY.
TRAIN ROBBING.

INMATE 17

FANCY JOHN HAWKS.
EMBEZZLEMENT.
EXTORTION.

INMATE 48

'KILLER' MCNAB.
MURDER. MORE MURDER.

INMATE 33

BILLY BOB WILLIAMSON.
LITTERING.

'These guys were bad enough when they were human.' Ant paled. 'We're not going to stand a chance against them now they've got claws and pointy teeth.'

Max stayed silent, staring at the posters for a long, long time.

'What have you spotted?' Ant asked.

'Something … I don't know …' Max shook his head. 'Maybe nothing.'

'Well, that's nice and vague.'

'Let's keep exploring.'

The next doors were much larger, double doors, and made of metal. The boys pushed them open and immediately scrabbling, squealing sounds erupted from the darkness.

'I hear rats!' Ant cried. 'Could this place get any worse?'

'Relax. They're all gone now.' Max looked round and whistled. 'This place is huge. I'll bet it was the prisoners' dining area.'

Wooden tables and benches sat in the middle of the vast room. The walls were solid stone with a kitchen built into one side. Max clocked a balcony above them, with a retractable ladder leading up to it.

'That must be where the wardens kept watch on the inmates while they were eating,' Max mused.

'I hate rats.' Ant huddled miserably near the door, between two large barrels. He knelt, scanning the ground. 'Where do you think they went?'

'Calm down. They must have taken off down this drain.' Max shone his light on a small round hole set in the floor. 'I suppose it was where the cooks sluiced the leftovers.' He glanced at Ant. 'Those are the slops barrels you're hiding behind, by the way.'

'Euuuugh!' Ant held his nose. 'I wondered what the smell was.'

'Don't worry. The rats are obviously more scared of us than we are of them.'

'Speak for yourself.'

'All right, let's get out of here,' Max grinned. 'I want to see where Fishbalm worked.'

The infirmary was through the last door they found. It was spotless inside, unlike the rest of the filthy rooms the boys had encountered. Shelves were laden with bottles and jars of unidentified liquids and the workbench was covered in tools, scalpels, medical implements and syringes. On one low table, the boys spotted a rack of test tubes. Stuck to each one was a label with *Pollen Extract* handwritten on it.

'Fishbalm wasn't lying.' Ant picked one up. 'He *does* have a serum to cure the beasts. Look, we're not achieving anything here, Max. Let's go back and get some sleep.'

'OK. You're right.' Max gave a resigned sigh. 'It's just … I know I'm missing something. Something important.'

They plodded back the way they had come. As they reached the stairs to their room, Max suddenly stopped. 'Of course!' He slapped his forehead. 'The answer was staring me in the face all along.'

'What answer? Stop being so cryptic.'

'I'll be back in ten minutes.' Max patted Ant's shoulder. 'There're a few things I need to do first.'

The others were asleep when Max finally crept back into the room. He silently slid between the sheets of his bed and put both hands behind his head.

'Yup,' he smiled. 'Staring me in the face all along.'

Chapter 7 – Under siege

Next morning, Dr Fishbalm burst into the study hauling a large sack behind him. 'Weapons!' he announced. 'Well … not exactly, but these are better than nothing.' He upended the sack and a pile of cricket equipment tumbled out. 'Some prisoners used to play during their exercise time,' he explained. 'I'd completely forgotten about it.'

'Cool!' Tiger began fastening on shin pads. 'At least my legs will be protected.'

The others dived into the pile. When the equipment was divided up, Max and Tiger carried bats, Cat had two spiked wicket stumps and Ant clutched a bag of rock-hard cricket balls.

'What about you, doctor?' Cat asked.

'I'm a bit of an amateur boxer.' Dr Fishbalm raised two skinny fists and did a quick shuffle on the carpet. 'A sneaky uppercut should lay low any beastie who wants to engage me in fisticuffs.' He pushed his top hat more firmly on his head. 'Shall we man the walls?' asked Dr Fishbalm.

'No.' Max folded his arms. 'I've got a better idea.'

'Say *what?*' said Tiger.

'This is a prison,' Max continued. 'Think about it. This place wasn't built to keep bad guys out. It was designed to keep them *in*.' He perched on the desk. 'Dr Fishbalm – how much of that antidote have you got?'

'Err …'

'You have a plan, don't you?' Ant butted in. 'I thought as much last night.'

'I do.' Max took Dr Fishbalm by the arm. 'You'd better sit down, doctor. There are a couple of things about our watches we neglected to mention, but they are functions that will come in very handy.'

And he told them his plan.

****

An hour later, the beasts attacked.

First they tried to scale the walls, climbing on each others' broad backs and pulling their companions up. The children and Dr Fishbalm raced around the ramparts, pushing them away with bats and stumps, until each precarious ladder of bodies collapsed in a growling heap. The monsters jumped back up, flexing their claws and growling menacingly.

'Is that all you've got?' Tiger jeered at the rampaging pack. 'We can keep this up all day!'

But the brutes had other ideas. A dozen appeared over the horizon, carrying a fallen tree-trunk. When they were a hundred yards away, they charged. The crude battering ram slammed into the gate and it shuddered on its hinges. They backed up and prepared for another run.

'Your turn, Ant!' Cat yelled.

Ant began to launch cricket balls at the assailants. He was an excellent shot. The balls bounced off the heads of the furious beasts and they retreated. One creature, larger than the others, roared at his reluctant accomplices. Cowed, his minions picked up the log and advanced again. Ant knocked three of them down but the others staggered on and slammed the battering ram into the gate again. The lock holding it shut began to crack.

The monsters howled in triumph. 'We have you now, hoomanssss!'

'They're almost in,' Max shouted. 'Everyone to their positions!'

Sensing victory, the creatures doubled their efforts. Twice as many as before grabbed the trunk and loped towards the prison entrance. Wood connected with metal and, with a tortured groan, the barrier burst open.

Cat, Ant and Tiger were caught in the open compound, eyes wide with fear. Without a sound, they turned and fled as the beasts poured through the gap and bounded after them.

The children raced into the main building, gibbering brutes hot on their heels. Ant spun, launched his last cricket ball and hit the lead pursuer. It collapsed with a grunt, tripping those following, until the corridor was filled with a squirming heap of bodies.

The children shot off again as the monsters scrambled to their feet. They reached the end of the corridor and raced through the open doors of the old prisoners' dining room. They climbed swiftly to the wardens' balcony and hauled the ladder up behind them.

The beasts poured into the dining room and clustered under the balcony, jumping up and down in a fruitless attempt to reach their prey.

'Come down hoomanssss,' they rasped. 'Come to ussss.'

Now the vast room was packed with agitated creatures screaming and pointing at the children.

When the last monster was inside the hall, Cat took a deep breath.

'Listen everyone,' she shouted at the top of her voice. 'We did not bring you here to fight, but to make peace!'

There was a frenzy of snarling. Tiger pounded the balcony rails with his cricket bat.

'Settle down, you lot!' he cried. 'You may as well hear what my friend has to say before you rip her to pieces.'

'Very tactful, Tiger,' Ant snorted.

But it worked. The hubbub died down, as the creatures squinted quizzically up at the children. Cat knew she had to have their undivided attention for the next two minutes.

'We have wonderful news!' She spread her arms wide. 'We can save everyone and return you to civilization.'

One beast, larger than the others, with a white stripe of fur cresting his head, stepped forwards. In a deep growling voice he said, 'How will you save usssss, girl?'

'We have made a miraculous discovery. One that will make you human again. You no longer have to sleep out in the open or eat raw meat.'

While she talked, Max and Dr Fishbalm eased themselves out of the slops barrels beside the door, the smell from the barrels obscuring their normal scent to avoid detection. The pair tiptoed from the hall, unnoticed by the beasts, who were still listening intently to Cat.

'Please let this work.' Max crossed his fingers and nodded to the doctor.

The pair swung the huge doors of the dining room shut with a clang. The monsters turned, disbelieving, as Max pushed the safety bar through the metal hoops on the door.

'Got them!' he whooped.

Chapter 8 – Double cross

Realizing they were trapped, the beasts flung themselves at the door, raking their talons down the metal surface. But it was no use. The barrier was simply too strong. Slowly, the malevolent beasts turned back round and looked up towards the children on the balcony. Ant gave a loud gulp.

'Tricky, tricky hoomanssss,' one breathed, grinding its broad jaws together. 'We will punisssssh you for thisssss …'

'You don't understand!' Cat cried. 'We trapped you here for your own good. We really do have an antidote for your condition! You'll be human again!'

To her horror, the creatures began to laugh, a phlegm-filled cackling that filled the hall. The leader silenced them with a raised paw.

'Hooman again?' he scoffed. 'Why would we wish that? Now we sleep under the starsssss. Know the thrill of the hunt.' He glanced dismissively around at his surroundings. 'You would take that away and return ussss to prison?'

'This isn't going quite how we'd hoped,' Ant whispered.

'We did not make very good hoomanssss.' For a second the creature sounded almost regretful. 'But we make excellent wolvesssss.'

The other creatures nodded in agreement.

'Now we will kill them,' one bellowed.

'Yesssss …' the others began to chant. 'Kill them. Kill them!'

What do I do now? Cat mouthed, panic in her eyes.

'Time for Plan B.' Ant stood up.

'Our friends are right outside the door, listening,' he yelled. 'It won't do you any good to kill us. You'll still be stuck in this room. But I have a solution.'

'What do you propose, hoomansss?' the leader rasped.

'Why don't we make a trade?' Ant suggested. 'Spare our lives and you'll get your freedom.'

The pack huddled together, grunting to each other. Finally the leader broke away.

'If you will take ussss to your transportation', he said, 'then yessss.'

'I don't get it. Why do you want to leave the island, if you like your new life so much?'

'Hunting sheep issss no challenge.' The leader gave a lupine grin. 'We wish to hunt ... everything.'

'So ... you'll definitely spare us if we provide you with a means to get off the island?' Ant asked.

'Yessss. Of course. We promise.'

'I get the feeling he's not to be trusted on that score,' Tiger commented.

'We don't exactly have a choice.' Ant began to lower the ladder.

'That's your favourite phrase, isn't it?'

'Unless you want to challenge them to a game of cricket, it's the only option we have.'

The children climbed down into the ring of creatures and stood back to back, shaking.

Ant watched as the wolf closest to him licked its lips with a slobbery red tongue.

'Tell your friendsssss to open the door,' the leader commanded.

'Let me check something first.' Cat pulled up her sleeve. 'What time is it, Tiger?'

'Erm. Shrinking time, I think.'

Simultaneously, the children pressed the buttons on their watches. The lead beast's bottom jaw fell open as the children shrank to micro-size. Cat, Ant and Tiger jumped into the sluice drain.

Listening to the cacophony of rage coming from inside the hall, Max gave a sigh. 'It sounds like they got away.'

'A truly excellent plan, my young friend.' Dr Fishbalm shook Max's hand. 'You would make a good criminal mastermind.' He chuckled to himself. 'That drain leads to a small stream right outside the prison. Let us depart. We can meet your companions there and proceed directly to the rip. And I have one bottle of explosive left to bring down the rocks and seal the rip forever.'

Cat, Ant and Tiger slid down the drain and landed in a sewage pipe, up to their knees in dirty liquid.

'I hope this is just water,' Tiger groaned, flicking on his torch. 'It doesn't smell too fresh.'

'Better than ending up as lunch.' Ant began to wade along the pipe behind Tiger, arms outstretched to stop himself falling over. 'Is it this way, Cat?'

There was silence behind him.

'Cat?'

'You said there were rats in the dining hall?' Cat whispered. 'What do you suppose they were eating all this time?'

'Scraps, I imagine. Left from when the prisoners use to have their meals there.'

'Scraps of mutton stew?'

'Yes.' Hairs stood up on the back of Ant's neck. 'Which ... would ... change them into mutants, too.'

He slowly turned. Cat was backing towards him. Beyond her, a scrawny rodent with incisors like chisels was crawling along the pipe. It may have been scrawny but the rat was bigger than they were, and its yellow eyes were glowing in the dim light.

'Oh no!' Ant's jaw dropped.

The children took off along the tunnel, but the

sludge they were wading through sucked at their shoes and slowed their pace. The rat had now been joined by two pack-mates and they crept steadily closer, making hideous hissing sounds to each other. Despite the children's frantic efforts, it was obvious that the rodents would attack long before they reached the sewer exit.

Max and Dr Fishbalm hurried down the corridor, on their way out of the prison. Suddenly, the doctor stopped.

'What's that noise?' he whispered.

'I don't hear anything.' Max tilted his head.

'It's coming from the cell in front of us.' The doctor took up a boxing stance. 'Have a quick peek, there's a good fellow.'

'And if there's a beast inside?'

'It will chase you out and I shall catch it unawares with a swift one, two.' He made a punching action in the air.

'I'm definitely not getting the best end of this deal.' Max slowly entered the cell, cricket bat raised.

'There's nothing here,' he called softly. 'You must be imagining things.'

There was a clink as the door swung shut and a key turned in the lock.

'What are you playing at, Fishbalm?' Max whirled around and grabbed the iron bars. 'Let me out!'

'I am truly sorry, my brave companion.' Dr Fishbalm's face was shrouded in shadows. 'For I harbour a real fondness for you and your friends. It's simply that I have a little scheme of my own, and I do not think you would approve of it.'

'I knew you were a phony.' Max glared at him. 'I *knew* it.'

'A phony? Oh no, I'm just misunderstood.'

'Does the antidote even work?'

'Of course, though it hasn't been properly tested.' Dr Fishbalm took off his hat and wiped the sweat from his brow. 'Anyway, must go. It's been nice chatting. Toodle pip.'

'Let me out!' Max shouted. 'It's not too late to do the decent thing!'

But Dr Amadeus Fishbalm had already gone.

Chapter 9 – Deception revealed

In the dining hall, the beasts' leader was instructing the rest of the pack. They had fetched giant stewing cauldrons, filled the containers to the brim with water from the kitchen and dragged them over to the tiny drain.

'Pour it all in,' he commanded. 'We will drown those lying hoomanssss.'

The beasts pawed at the cauldrons, tipping them over.

'They will be the ones who die in thisssss prison. Not usssss.'

Cat, Ant and Tiger stumbled along the pipe, exhausted. The rats, sensing the weakness of their prey, began to close the gap.

At that moment, Tiger tripped and landed face-down in the putrid water.

'Get up!' Cat yelled.

The lead rat was almost upon Tiger. It opened its jaws ready to bite. Just then, it turned its massive head. There was a noise thundering down the drain towards them.

While its head was turned, Tiger scrambled to his feet. The rodents gave a squeal of terror as a colossal wave of water surged along the pipe.

'Uh, oh!' said Ant. 'Prepare to get wet!'

'I already am wet,' moaned Tiger.

'I mean *wetter.*'

The wave crashed behind them, sweeping both the rats and the children up in a foaming torrent. They shot along the conduit, a mass of fur and flesh, bouncing off the uneven surface – until they tumbled out of the exit pipe and landed in a stream. The children swam for the bank and dragged themselves on to the grass, wet clothes plastered to their bodies. The rats paddled towards them, teeth still bared, unwilling to give up on their quarry.

The children quickly activated their watches and grew to normal size.

'Ouch!' Tiger slapped a furry body off his leg. 'The nasty vermin bit me!'

'You sure you want to take us on, Ratty?' Ant raised an eyebrow. 'We're pretty big now.'

The rat did not. With a dismayed squeak, it scurried away and plunged back into the water.

'No sign of Max and the doctor.' Tiger looked around. 'They ought to be here by now. Should we wait?'

'There's no need.' Cat was wringing out the bottom of her t-shirt. 'The ground is so soft, they'll be able to follow our footprints. I want to get to the rip as quickly as possible and find Max's watch, so we can finally get out of here.'

'I second that.' Tiger set off. 'Let's go. *Tout de suite!*'

An hour and a half later, the children reached the rip. Cat and Ant sat on a large rock next to the portal, trying to dry out their soggy clothes in the sun.

Tiger remained standing. 'I'll go find Max's watch,' he said, hobbling away. 'The ditch he fell in is just round the back of those rocks.'

'Are you all right?' Cat looked concerned. 'You're limping.'

'I'm sure Fishbalm will fix me up.' Tiger shrugged. 'He is a doctor, after all.' He vanished behind the rocks.

'What's taking Max and Fishbalm so long?' Ant stood up and peered across the moor. 'Wait a minute! I see someone.'

Cat scrambled to her feet. A lanky figure in

elevated headgear was marching towards them. She looked through the magnifier on her watch. 'It's Dr Fishbalm.' She bit her lip. 'But there's no sign of Max.'

Dr Fishbalm finally reached them and flopped down beside them, breathing heavily. 'That was quite a trek,' he wheezed. 'No wonder the beasts couldn't find this place.'

'Where's Max, Dr Fishbalm?' Cat sat next to him. 'What happened?'

'I have locked Max in a cell in the prison.' Dr Fishbalm pulled a key from his pocket and handed it to her. 'You may now go and get him, while the creatures are still safely locked in the dining hall.'

'*What?*' Cat was aghast.

He patted her hand listlessly. 'My sincerest apologies, but when you return I fear I shall be gone.'

'I don't understand.'

'I do not think you will allow me to travel through the rip, especially since you require me to seal it behind you.' Dr Fishbalm would not look up to meet her eye. 'Yet I cannot do that, for I must escape this island, too.'

'Max was right all along,' Ant spat. 'You weren't really helping us. You just wanted to use the rip yourself. We should never have trusted someone who looks like a failed magician.'

'To my eternal shame, I am afraid that is true.' Dr Fishbalm twiddled his moustache.

'But you *can* get off the island!' Cat protested. 'You have the prisoners trapped for now and an antidote to make them human again. All you have to do is contact the authorities and they'll come and rescue you.'

'I'm afraid it is not as simple as that.'

'Oh, it's very simple.' Max stepped out from behind a rock, holding a cricket bat. 'Bet you're surprised to see me, huh?'

'What? I don't …' Dr Fishbalm spluttered. 'How did you get out of your cell?'

'A master key.' Max held up a shining metal key. 'I found it in the Head Warden's office last night. I had a feeling you'd pull a stunt like this, so I figured it would come in handy.'

'But ... how could you possibly know I'd betray you?' The doctor threw up his hands. 'I thought I came across as quite charming.'

'I'm a bit of an amateur detective.' Max smiled thinly. 'Why would a man of your obvious talents end up a prison doctor in the middle of nowhere? Why would the wardens leave without giving you weapons?' He wagged a finger at Dr Fishbalm. 'Most importantly, why would you build a balloon unless it was a desperate attempt to get off this island? With the boat gone, it was your only option. We just arrived before you'd had a chance to use it.'

Max pulled a piece of paper from his pocket and unfolded it. 'Then I saw a patch of empty wall in the Head Warden's office, where a poster had been taken down.' He handed it to Cat. 'The "doctor" folded it to hide the writing, then put it in a frame in the dining room.'

'I'm afraid my own arrogance has caused my downfall,' Dr Fishbalm said quietly.

Cat read it, her face paling.

INMATE 10

DR AMADEUS FISHBALM
PROFESSIONAL CONFIDENCE TRICKSTER

'If the authorities ever come back, they'll just lock him up with the other inmates. You see, he was only pretending that he was the prison doctor.' Max rubbed his cheek wearily. 'He was actually one of the *prisoners*.'

Chapter 10 – Tiger?

'I believe I am finally unmasked.' Dr Fishbalm stared at his feet. 'It's true. I was an inmate here as well. I only avoided changing into a beast because, like the wardens, I never ate any of the stew.' He put his head in his hands. 'I do not approve of killing in any form, not even animals, which is why I am a vegetarian. It's what stopped me changing into a beast.'

'Just goes to show there's good in everyone,' Ant said. The others glared at him. 'Sorry. I'll shut up.'

'You're right, Max. If I cure the inmates it won't do *me* any good,' Dr Fishbalm lamented. 'The authorities won't care, for all criminals receive a life sentence without parole. If I don't get off this island then, one way or another, I'll be stuck here forever.'

'I don't think I like this world very much,' Ant said.

'No.' Dr Fishbalm agreed. 'Neither do I.' He clasped his hands together, pleading to the children. 'Won't you please let me go through the rip? I'll admit I've been less than gentlemanly, but I didn't actually hurt anyone.'

'I trusted you,' said Cat angrily. 'I defended you.'

'Yes. You are an excellent young lady.' Dr Fishbalm looked soulfully at her. 'You surely wouldn't leave me to rot here.'

'Want to bet?'

'Yeah.' Max tapped the cricket bat against his palm. 'Don't you dare go near that rip.'

'You're missing the point, Dr Fishbalm,' Ant said. 'We need you to bring down the overhang and seal the rip. The bar on the dining room door won't hold forever and then the monsters will be loose again. If they find this place and escape into another dimension, there will be carnage!'

'Then our discussion is over.' Dr Fishbalm picked up his bag. 'I shall do my best to hide the rip using foliage. But, once you are gone, I *will* use it to escape.' He got up and shuffled away. 'I really do apologize, but you leave me no choice. Still, I shall remove myself until you have departed.'

'Let him go.' Max lowered the cricket bat. He looked around. 'Where's Tiger?'

'He's gone to find your watch.'

'As soon as he gets back, we'll be out of here.' He tried to put on a brave face. 'Perhaps Fishbalm will have a change of heart, though I seriously doubt it.'

'I can't believe I was so wrong about him,' Cat moaned. 'He seemed such a nice man.'

'If I was in his shoes, I might have tried to escape, too. This isn't exactly a holiday destination,' said Ant.

'Go find Tiger before Fishbalm decides he wants your watch as well,' Cat said. 'I'll keep guard here.'

'Are you sure?'

'Fishbalm won't try to get past me,' she insisted. 'Not in the mood I'm in. Besides, he may be a con man but I'm pretty certain he wouldn't hurt me. Not when all he has to do is wait for us to leave then follow us through the rip.'

'All right.' Max handed her the bat. 'We'll be back as fast as possible. C'mon, Ant.'

The two boys vanished round the outcrop. Cat leant against a rock, sulking. She could see Dr Fishbalm sitting on a flat stone further down the hill. He kept trying to catch her eye, but she ignored him. Eventually, he moved even further away.

Cat heard a noise to her left, soft footprints crunching on bracken.

'You took your time, Tiger,' she said, staring at her feet. 'Max and Ant have gone looking for you.'

'Hello, hooman.' The voice was low and gruff. 'I followed your footprintssss.'

Cat's head shot up. A beast was crawling through the grass towards her. It smiled broadly, revealing two rows of jagged canines.

'I am ssssoooo hungry. The others will not let me hunt with them.'

Cat began to back away, clutching the bat. The monster's jaws clicked together, as if it had a nervous tic.

'Yesssss.' It tensed itself, ready to pounce. 'Sssooooo hungry.'

Cat swung the bat as the creature leapt at her, but the brute seized the wood between its teeth and tore it from her grasp. Spitting the bat out, it rose above her and opened its mouth wide, drool dripping from its fangs.

'Oh, no.' Cat covered her eyes.

She felt a hand grab her arm and fling her sideways. She landed on the grass a few feet away and scrambled into a sitting position.

Dr Amadeus Fishbalm stood between her and the creature, skinny legs apart and fists raised in a boxing stance.

'Don't you *dare* lay a hand on this child,' he threatened. 'If you want her you'll have to dispose of me first.'

'Suit yoursssself,' the beast leered. It crouched down on its haunches and dug splayed feet into the soft ground for better purchase. Then it leapt at the doctor.

Dr Fishbalm did a quick sidestep, swung round and elbowed the attacker on the back of the neck. It sprawled across the ground but was on its feet in an instant. With a backhanded swipe it sent the doctor flying. Grinning malevolently, the beast turned its attention to Cat again.

Cat screamed as the creature reached out towards her with its yellowing claws. But, just as she thought she was done for, the beast sagged as Dr Fishbalm landed on its back, one torn sleeve fastening round its thick neck. Blood was seeping from Dr Fishbalm's nose but he held on while the brute thrashed in an attempt to throw him off.

'Run, Cat!' he shouted.

But she was too terrified to move. She could only watch as the beast ducked its head, trying to claw at the unwelcome passenger. Dr Fishbalm held on all the more tightly. With a supreme effort, the creature finally shook him off. The doctor landed on his feet and danced away, as the monster lashed out, narrowly missing his torso.

'Time for a taste of your own medicine!' Dr Fishbalm did a quick shuffle and punched the creature on its snout. 'Take that!'

The beast didn't even flinch.

'Oh.' The doctor's eyes widened.

The creature backhanded him again and he flew through the air, crashing into a gorse bush and flopping to the ground with a groan.

Cat raced over and flung herself down beside him.

'Get up!' she cried, shaking his arm. 'Please!'

'Two snacksssss instead of one,' the beast chuckled, advancing on them. 'Thissss issss a good hunt.'

It leaned over Cat, salivating, so close she could smell rotting meat on its fetid breath.

'Get your dirty pawsssss off my palsssss!' a voice roared from above.

Cat looked up through splayed fingers. Another beast was perched on top of the outcrop. But this one was smaller than the other creatures she had encountered and wore a familiar outfit. The dial of a watch sparkled in the weak sunlight, strapped to one hairy wrist.

'Tiger?' she choked. 'Is that you?'

With an inhuman howl, Tiger jumped from the outcrop. As he descended, the other creature leapt to meet him. They collided in mid-air with a sickening thud and landed in a pile of twisted arms and legs. They writhed across the grass, locked in a deadly embrace, each trying to get on top of the other and deliver a fatal blow.

'Found the watch!' Max and Ant appeared round the rocks, holding up the device.

'Found Tiger!' said Cat pointing towards the fighting bodies.

The boys stopped dead in their tracks.

'What on earth …?' said Ant.

'Don't just stand there chaps.' Dr Fishbalm got groggily to his feet and grabbed his hat. 'Your friend needs some assistance.'

In his hand he had a vial of blue liquid.

'Hold that horrible beast down,' said Dr Fishbalm. 'And stay away from its claws.'

'Which one?'

'The bigger one,' Cat urged.

With all three of them helping, and with Tiger's new beast-like strength, they finally pinned the larger creature to the ground.

'Hold its jaws open.' Dr Fishbalm was dancing around in agitation. 'Mind the teeth, too. One bite and it will infect you.'

Max managed to get the creature's mouth open and the doctor poured half the liquid down its throat.

The brute began to convulse. With a final effort, it threw off the children and staggered away. The creature that had once been Tiger remained on all fours, looking suspiciously at his former companions.

'What hassss happened to me?' he asked plaintively. 'I am hungry.'

'You've obviously been bitten by something that has passed its mutation on to you.' Dr Fishbalm slowly approached the boy. 'But do not worry. I have just enough antidote left for you.'

'The rat,' Ant paled. 'He was bitten by a rat.'

'That explains everything.' Dr Fishbalm slowly held out the vial. 'I can make you normal again, Tiger, never fear.'

'I do not wish to be normal.' Tiger shook his shaggy head. 'I like thisssss. I am fassst. I am strong. Jusssst leave me be.'

'Then you will be alone when your friends go through the rip.' The doctor knelt in front of him. 'As I have been for a long, long time.' He wiped a tear from his eye. 'Believe me, young man. You really do not want that.'

'I will live with the otherssss when they get free.'

Tiger tapped his lip with a pointed talon. 'I will know absolute freedom, asssss they do.'

'You will know only misery.' A man in ragged clothes appeared behind them. 'For they were monsters long before they took on the physical appearance of such. Unless you are a criminal, they will not accept you. Just as they rejected me.'

'Very sage advice, Mr Wattbottle.' Dr Fishbalm kept his eyes on Tiger.

'The handyman?' said Cat.

'The very same,' said Wattbottle.

'I suspected it might be you, though it was hard to tell under all that fur.'

'You were correct. And thank you for curing me.' Mr Wattbottle gave a small bow. 'I, for one, am delighted to be returned to my proper form.'

He clasped his hands together and knelt before Tiger. 'Please take the antidote, hairy young man, before your basest instincts take over and you end up howling at the moon without knowing why.'

Tiger's jowls trembled. Then he held out a shaking paw. 'Passss it here before I change my mind.'

Dr Fishbalm handed him the vial and he downed it in one gulp.

The others watched in astonishment as he slowly morphed back into the boy they knew.

'That was ...' he took a deep breath, '*hairy.*'

Cat groaned, then smiled. 'Good to have you back.'

Tiger rubbed his stomach. 'I'm starving.'

'I have a cauliflower sandwich in my pocket for the trip,' Dr Fishbalm volunteered.

'Yeah. I'm not *that* hungry. Can we go now?'

Dr Fishbalm pulled miserably at his moustache. He got up and paced up and down, mumbling to himself. He looked longingly at the rip, only a few feet away. Finally, he sat down again.

'Begone.' He waved the children away. 'I will seal the rip behind you. Having witnessed this altercation, I cannot let those creatures find the rip and pass through it. You are correct. They must be contained here.'

'Won't they tear you apart?' Tiger asked. 'You've really ticked them off.'

'Very tactful, Tiger.' Cat pulled a face at her friend.

'Mr Wattbottle and I will keep them contained until the authorities arrive and administer the antidote. Then I will go back to jail.' He gave a wan smile. 'Though I do not know how long I shall survive there. As Tiger so eloquently put it, I have really ticked them off.'

'I knew you weren't all bad!' Cat flung her arms around the astonished man. 'Max, we can't just leave him here. Mr Wattbottle can seal the rip instead, can't he?'

'I don't know.' Max rubbed his chin. 'Fishbalm's still a con man.'

'I have no idea what you are all talking about,' Mr Wattbottle interrupted. 'But am I right in understanding that Dr Fishbalm invented an antidote to my curse?'

'He did,' said Ant.

'And he trapped the creatures in the prison?'

'With a little help from us,' added Tiger.

'And he risked his life to save you.'

'He certainly did,' said Cat.

'Then in my lowly opinion', Mr Wattbottle said, 'I feel he has fully paid his debt to society.'

'Unfortunately, I don't think the authorities will agree,' Dr Fishbalm said sadly.

'The same authorities who couldn't be bothered trying to rescue me?' Mr Wattbottle raised a bushy eyebrow. 'Well, I may only be a handyman, but I know right from wrong.' He gave a sly smile. 'I also know how to build a boat.'

'A boat!' Dr Fishbalm gave a delighted grin. 'I never even tried to construct one in case the monsters hijacked it at the jetty!' He shrugged. 'Besides, I'm not much of a carpenter.'

'That's a bit ironic,' Max sniffed. 'Since it's the one skill you actually needed.'

Mr Wattbottle grinned. 'I, on the other hand, happen to be a pretty good carpenter.'

'What are you saying?' Dr Fishbalm could barely contain his glee. 'That you'll build me a boat?'

'It's the least I can do,' Mr Wattbottle nodded. 'I'll wait until you set sail before I contact the authorities. When they finally arrive … I'll claim I never saw you.'

'And, in return, I will never con anyone again! I have learned my lesson.'

'Then I shall let you say goodbye to your companions.' Mr Wattbottle patted Cat on the head. 'A pleasure to make your acquaintance, young lady, however briefly. Sorry I tried to eat you.'

And he strolled off, humming to himself.

'I shall go and fetch my explosives to seal the rip,' said Dr Fishbalm. He knelt in front of Cat. 'I assume you will not be here when I return but, rest assured, I shall never forget you.'

'You'd better not.' Cat smiled at him. 'Good luck and thank you.'

'No. Thank *you*.' Dr Fishbalm tipped his hat at her. 'For teaching a monster how to be a man again. I wish you every luck in your endeavours. Though, from what you have told me of your enemy, you have a hard road ahead.'

Then he was off and running after Mr Wattbottle. Every few yards he leapt in the air and clicked his heels. Cat waved until he was out of sight then she turned back to her friends.

'You've gotta like that guy.' Tiger grinned. 'Despite everything. He's got style.'

'He certainly does,' Cat giggled.

'Are you sure we're doing the right thing, letting him escape the island?' Max pursed his lips. 'He was a criminal, after all.'

'Yes,' said Cat firmly. She tucked a strand of hair behind her ear. 'If there's one thing this island taught me, it's that people can change. Literally.'

'Good enough for me.' Max nodded. 'I guess everyone deserves a second chance.'

'Got her!' Cat shrieked. Vilana's signal was finally evident on her watch and they could resume the chase.

'Shall we?' Ant pointed to the rip.

The others nodded and synchronized their watches to the same coordinates as Cat's.

'I'm betting our next destination has a beach,' said Tiger. 'With palm trees. And hammocks.'

'And if it doesn't?'

Tiger grinned. 'Then I'll become an amateur hammock maker.'

NEXT ... The Scorpion Legion